A guide to writing Excel formulas and VBA macros

Mark McIlroy

www.markmcilroy.com

ISBN 978-1530079445

Edition 6

Other books by the author

Introduction to the Stockmarket

The Wise Investor

SQL Essentials

The Art and Craft of Computer Programming

Contents

1. Introduction

As the title suggests this book is an introduction to writing Excel formulas and macros.

The book assumes only a basic familiarity with Excel.

The book is not intended to be a comprehensive guide to Excel. Excel is a complex system that has many functions, many of them are rarely used.

The book covers the most commonly used functions, and includes everything you need to know to write basic or advanced formulas and macros.

This book is in a condensed format. You will need to read each section in turn and then experiment with formulas that are similar to the examples that are presented in the text.

This book is based on Excel 2013, however the material is relevant to most versions of Excel.

2. Section A – Excel Formulas

2.1 Introduction to Excel formulas

Let's start with a few basics.

As you probably know, every cell on the worksheet page is referred to by a reference such as D7.

The letter refers to the cell column (as shown along the top of the worksheet area), and the number refers to the cell row (as shown down the left hand side of the worksheet area).

Now, enter the value 100 in cell A1, which is the cell at the top-left of the worksheet area.

Go to cell B3 and type in the value "=A1".

As you can see, the value 100 is now also displayed in cell B3.

If you change the value in cell A1 to 200, say, you can see that the value in cell B3 is automatically updated.

Very basic, but this is an Excel formula.

2.2 Referring to other cells

There are three ways to refer to other cells in Formulas: "Absolute" references, "Relative" references and "names".

Names are discussed in a later section in this book.

Relative references have the format =A1

Absolute references have the format =$A$1

Both formulas produce exactly the same results. The difference appears when you copy-and-paste a formula to a different area of a worksheet.

When you copy-and-paste, the relative references are modified to match the new position of the formula on the worksheet.

This is very useful and allows you to copy a formula into a large number of cells, and have it automatically updated.

Absolute references such as =$A$1 are left unchanged when the formula is copy-and-pasted to a different area of a worksheet.

It is also possible to enter a value where only the rows are updated, such as =$A1, or when only the columns are updated such as =A$1. These forms are not widely used however they are quite useful once you are familiar with them..

A useful feature of Excel is that, when you are editing a formula, if you press the F4 key Excel will change the cell reference you are on from a Relative reference to an Absolute reference or vice versa, which saves a lot of typing dollar signs.

Finally it is possible to refer to cells on a different worksheet to the one you are currently working on.

If the other worksheet is in the same workbook, these references have the form =SheetName1!A1

If the other worksheet is in a different workbook, these references have the form ='[WorkSheetName]SheetName1'!A1

In practice the easiest way to use these references is to type = in the new cell, then click the mouse on the target cell and Excel will automatically generate the entire reference for you.

I would generally recommend against referring to cells in anther workbook. Over time file names change and files are moved, which means that links of this type are often broken. It can then be difficult to determine what how a worksheet with broken links is supposed to work.

Referring to different sheets in the same workbook is fine.

2.3 Basic operations

The basic operations in an Excel formula are listed below.

+   Addition
-        Subtraction
*   Multiplication
/   Division
^   Exponentiation
()   Brackets

An example of a Excel formula is =A1 + (A2 / A3)

Try entering this formula in cell B3 and typing in values in cells A1, A2 and A3.

2.4 Basic functions

Excel contains a large number of functions. Descriptions of these can be found in the Excel help or on various websites (See the Resources section later in this book).

The most useful functions are listed below

ABS()   Returns the absolute value of a number

SUM()   Returns the total of a set of values

AVERAGE() Returns the average of a set of values

MIN()   Returns the minimum value of two values

MAX()   Returns the maximum value of two values

ROUND()   Rounds a value to a specified number of decimal places.

For example, =MAX(ABS(A1) * 0.001, 19.95) will return the value that is 0.1% of cell A1 or 19.95, whichever is greater.

Range formulas such as SUM() require a range cell reference.

This is entered in the form A1:A10, for example =SUM(A1:A10). This formula example will add up all the values in the cells A1 through to A10 and display the value in the cell that has the formula in it.

As with single cell references you can use Absolute or Relative references in your ranges.

2.5 Logical operators

Excel allows you to enter 'Logical' operators in cells.

These are listed below

IF(formula1, formula2, formula3)

AND(formula1, formula 2)

OR(formula1, formula 2)

The 'IF" operator allows you to test a condition and return a different result depending on different conditions.

For example =IF(A1 > 10, 10, A1)

This formula will test the value of cell A1. If it is greater than 10, the result returned will be 10, otherwise the result will be the value of cell A1.

Another example, =IF(AND(A1 > 10, B1 < 20), 10, A1)

As you can see these formulas are starting to get a little complicated. However if you work on a lot of spreadsheets you will eventually have to write formulas such as these.

The example above tests the values of both cells A1 and B1. If A1 is greater than 10 and B1 is less than 20, then the result of the formula will be 10, otherwise it will be the value of cell A1.

These operations can be nested to multiple levels in a single formula. If you are going to nest 'IF' statements they must be in the following form

=IF(condition1, result1, IF(condition2, result2, IF(condition3, result3, result4)))

2.6 Names

In addition to Absolute and Relative references, you can also refer to other cells in formulas by giving the cell a name.

This can simply complex spreadsheets, particularly when you are using several worksheets within a single workbook.

To give a cell a name, click on the cell, right click, and select 'Define Name'.

Then type in a name for the cell and click ok.

For example, define a name for the cell A1 as Fee_rate

You can then type formulas anywhere within the workbook using a syntax such as

    =Fee_rate * 2

2.7 Table lookup functions

The next functions to consider are the table lookup functions.

These functions are VLOOKUP() and HLOOKUP() and are very useful.

I will focus on VLOOKUP() as it is more widely used.

The VLOOKUP() function allows you to search a table of results and extract an entry.

For example,

    VLOOKUP(A1, $D$1:$E$100, 3, FALSE)

This formula assumes that the current worksheet has a table of figures in cells D1 to E100.

The formula will search the first column of the table for the value in cell A1, and if it finds a matching entry in the table it will return the value in the 3rd column of the table into the result cell.

The final parameter will usually be FALSE, which specifies that an exact match must be found in the table. A value of TRUE in this parameter will result in the next best entry being found in an approximate search.

2.8 Goal Seek

Excel contains a "Goal seek" function. This is found on the Data – What If Analysis menu.

Goal seek allows you to change a model to produce a certain value, by having Excel automatically modify an input value.

For example, say that you produce a financial model in Excel that models the income a client can receive in retirement from their retirement funds.

You want to select the maximum income that your client can draw from their retirement fund, such that their funds will last until they are 90 years of age.

To achieve this, set up a spreadsheet with the income drawn each year and the declining balance of their retirement fund.

Then run a "Goal Seek" function, targeting the fund balance at age 90 cell to zero, by modifying the income drawn each year cell.

2.9 Solver

Solver is a more powerful version of the 'Goal seek' function.

Solver enables Excel to search for the minimum or maximum value that a model can produce, by varying one or more input cells.

You can also specify 'constraints', which involve the minimum or maximum values that are allowed in various cells within the model when Excel is searching for a solution.

Solver is not installed by default. To activate Solver, click File, Options, Add-Ins, Go, tick the 'Solver Add-In' box and click ok.

Now you should see 'Solver' on the Data menu.

Please note that having Solver activated may slow down Excel when starting up, so it is probably a good idea to only install it when you are actually using it.

The Solver screen is fairly self-explanatory.

2.10 Pivot tables

It is beyond the scope of this book to give a comprehensive review of pivot tables.

However an introduction is in order.

If you have a set of data, such as a set of financial transactions, Excel can summarise your data into a table.

This is done using the functionality known as a Pivot Table.

For example, you can produce a table that has one row for each month, with totals for that month, and a total for the year, from a large number of input transactions.

The Pivot Table functionality is relatively complex and varies with each version of Excel.

3. Part B – Writing VBA Macros

3.1 Setup up Excel for macros

There are a few preliminary steps that must be taken before you can start writing VBA macros.

First that you must add the "Developer" option to the Excel main menu. This option is not turned on by default.

To start, open a new blank worksheet.

Then click the following options

  File

  Options

  Customise Ribbon

This sequence will display a large box with several panes in it. In the right-hand pane, find the entry labelled "Developer" and click on the box to place a tick in the box. Click OK.

You should then be back on the new blank worksheet, however the word "Developer" should now appear on the Excel menu bar.

3.2 VBA Macros

You are now ready to write your first VBA macro.

Click on the Excel menu bar "Developer" and then click on "Visual Basic"

This sequence will bring up the Excel VBA development environment.

Click on "Insert" on the top menu bar then click on "Module"

This should bring up a blank window, ready for you to write a VBA macro.

Type in the following text

```
Public Function my_test_macro( param1 as double )

      my_text_macro = param1 * 2

End function
```

Now click File on the menu bar and then "Save"

This will bring up the file Save dialog box.

Note that at this point you must click on the 'Save As Type" drop-down list and select "Excel Macro-Enabled Workbook" BEFORE you enter a file name, select a folder and click Save.

After saving, Excel will return you to the VBA development screen.

Now you can click "File" on the menu bar and click on "Close and return to Microsoft Excel".

Now, on the blank worksheet, type 100 in to cell A1.

Then type the following formula into any cell

```
=my_test_macro( A1 )
```

Now you should see the value 200 in your new cell.

Congratulations – a working VBA macro of your own design.

3.3 Returning a value from your function

As you can see from the previous simple example, you return a value from your VBA macro function into the calling worksheet by assigning a value to the function name using the '=' operator, for example:

```
function_name = value
```

In this example, the value of the variable 'value' will be returned into the cell of the calling worksheet.

3.4 Parameters

Most macros will have at least one parameter. This is the list of names after the word 'Function' and the name of the function.

Excel VBA is a line based language. This means that each statement must be on a separate line. Each statement must start and finish on a single line. If you want to continue an individual statement on to the next line, place space and an underscore "_" at the end of the line.

For example

```
Public Function my_test_macro(    param1 as double, _
                                  param2 as double, _
                                  param3 as string)

End Function
```

Take note of the position of every item, including commas. Computer software is demanding and each item must be entered exactly as defined by the language.

The value entered after the word "As" is the type of the parameter.

The most commonly used types are the word "double", which represents a numeric value, and "string" which represents a short item of text.

The word "double" is shorthand for "double precision floating point variable". This is accurate to approximately 15 digits of precision.

There is also a data type "single" which is accurate to approximately 7 digits of accuracy. Single precision data was originally used by programmers to save computer memory but there is no practical reason in the modern world to use this data type.

Parameters can be used in expressions to calculate values.

For example,

```
Option Explicit

Public Function my_test_macro( param1 as double, param2 as double )

     my_test_macro = param1 * param2

End Function
```

You can test this change to your new macro by entering it as shown, saving the VBA macro screen, and entering the following in a cell on your new worksheet.

```
=my_test_macro( A1, A2 )
```

If you enter values into the cells A1 and A2 the multiplication result of your two values should appear in the cell that you entered the formula in.

The words 'Option Explicit" at the top of your macro file tells Excel to demand that all the variable you use in your code are properly declared. It helpful to include this statement.

If you want to change the value of a parameter within your function, it is good programming practice to use the word "ByVal" before the parameter definition to indicate that you only want to use the parameter value in your function, you are not attempting to change its value in the source worksheet.

For example

```
Public Function my_test_macro(   ByVal param1 as double, _
                                 param2 as double)

     param1 = param1 / 100

     my_test_macro = param1 * param2

End Function
```

3.5 Expressions

VBA expressions follow the natural path that is familiar from mathematical expressions.

For example

```
my_test_macro = (param1 * param2) / param3 + 10
```

The operators are

+	Addition
-	Subtraction
*	Multiplication
/	Division
^	Exponentiation
()	Brackets
&	Concatenate two strings, i.e. add one to the end of the other

A wide range of build-in mathematic functions is available, see the "Resources" section at the end of this book.

You can get help on a function by highlighting its name in a VBA code window and pressing F1

Some examples are

Abs(param1)   return the absolute value of a number

Sqr(param1)   return the square root of a number

Log(param1)   return the natural logarithm (base 'e') of a number

```
result = Abs( Log( param1 ) + param2 )
```

An example of a string expression is

```
formal_name = last_name & ", " & first_name
```

3.6 Local variables

Once your calculations get a little more complex you will need to use "local variables".

These are values that are defined only within a single function.

For example, modify your test macro to the following code.

```
Public Function my_test_macro(    param1 as double, param2 as double )

        Dim value1 as double
        Dim value2 as double

        value1 = param1 * param2
```

```
        my_test_macro = value1

    End Function
```

The value of these variables "value1" and "value2" only applies within the boundaries of the Function and End Function keywords of this function.

You can use the same names in a different macro function, in which case they will have separate values from your first function.

By now you have probably noticed that many of the keywords in VBA seem to have almost meaningless names.

VBA, more formally called Visual Basic for Applications, builds on a long history of the BASIC language stretching back to the 1960's.

Many of the keywords are based on historical meanings.

For example, the word 'Dim' which is used for declaring local variables is short for the word "Dimension', which was initially used to specify the dimensions of an array.

3.7 Data types

The main data types that you will need to use are "double", "integer", and "string".

The "double" data type can represent any practical number, including a decimal part.

The "integer" data type can only represent whole numbers, but should be used when you declare a variable that will only hold whole numbers, such as the number of times to repeat a loop.

A "string" is a small piece of text, such as a name. String values have double quotes around them, such as the code below

```
    client_name = "Fred Smith"
```

3.8 Comments

You can enter comments within your code files that are intended for a human reader, and are ignored by the program system.

This is done by typing a single quote character.

Anything after the quote character to the end of the line will be displayed in green and is ignored by Excel when it is executing your code.

For example:

```
'
' Written by Mark McIlroy, 15/02/16
'
' This is a test function
'
' The result is the value param1 * param2
'

        Public Function my_test_macro(    param1 as double, _
                                          param2 as double, _
                                          param3 as string)

            Dim value1 as double
            Dim value2 as double

            value1 = param1 * param2        ' main calculation

            my_test_macro = value1

        End Function
```

Comments are extremely useful when you come back to modify the code on a future date, or when some other person needs to work on your code.

3.9 Constants

As you do more programming you will find that you use fixed values quite often.

There is a way to specify fixed values within your code so that they are easier to read and modify. This is done with 'constants'

Constants are specified by placing code in this format at the top of the code window.

```
Const CONSTANT_NAME As DATA_TYPE = VALUE
```

For example

```
Const CURRENT_MODELS_NAME As String = "Portfolios 17.11.2015.xlsm"
```

You can then use this name in your code in the place of the actual value, such as the code below:

```
workbook_name = CURRENT_MODELS_NAME
```

Constants make your code easier to read and modify and reduces the chance of bugs occurring in your code. It is recommended that everywhere you use a constant value you declare it at the top of the file.

3.10 IF statements

The VBA code that we have looked at so far uses variables, functions and mathematical operators.

However thus far you probably could have used a standard Excel worksheet to produce the same results.

The following sections identify the more powerful features of VBA.

An 'if' statement allows you to test a condition.

For example consider the macro code below

```
If param1 > 10 Then
        my_test_macro = 10
End If
```

You can also specify an alternative expression, such as the code below.

```
If param1 > 10 Then
        my_test_macro = 10
Else
        my_test_macro = 20
End If
```

This statement will compare the value of param1 to 10, and if it is greater than ten it will set your result to 10, otherwise it will set it to 20.

It is also possible to chain 'if' statements into longer sets of statements such as the example below

```
If param1 > 10 and param1 < 20 Then
        my_test_macro = 10
Else
        my_test_macro = 20

ElseIf param1 >= 20 and param1 < 30 Then

        my_test_macro = 30

ElseIf param1 >= 30 and param1 < 40 Then
```

```
        my_test_macro = 40
Else
        my_test_macro = 50

    End If
```

3.11 Boolean expressions

'If' statements and 'while' loops (which we will see further on) use what is known as 'boolean' expressions.

The Boolean operators are

a = b	equal
a <> b	not equal
a < b	less than
a <= b	less than or equal to
a > b	greater than
a >= b	greater than or equal to
a And b	both TRUE
a Or b	either one TRUE
Not a	if a is FALSE

You can declare variables that will the True or False using a statement as below

```
Dim found as Boolean
```

Some developers prefer to use integer variables which have the same effect, such as

```
Dim found as Integer
```

You can then use statements similar to the ones below

```
found = False

If not found then
        ' insert code here
End If
```

3.12 While loops

You can repeat a section of code using a construct known as a 'while' loop.

This has the general form below

```
While expression
        ' code here
Wend
```

For example

```
count = 0

While count < 10
        ' code here

        count = count + 1
Wend
```

The code inside this example loop would be executed 10 times

3.13 For loops

There are several loop statements in VBA.

The most commonly used are the 'while' loop and the 'for' loop.

The 'for' loop has the general form

```
For variable = expression1 To expression2

      ' code here

Next
```

For an example see the code below

```
For r = 1 To 1000

        ' code here

Next
```

In this example, the code inside the loop will be executed 1000 times

Loops can be 'nested' inside each other in any combination, such as in the example below.

```
For day = 1 to 31
      For account = 1 to 100
            ' code here
      Next
Next
```

You should be aware that code inside nested loops can be execute an large number of times, so this may slow your system down somewhat.

In the following example, the code inside the inner loop will be executed 1,000,000 times.

```
For a = 1 to 1000
      For b = 1 to 1000
            ' code here
      Next
Next
```

3.13 Using worksheet functions

VBA has a fairly limited number of mathematical functions.

A much wider range of functions is available by accessing the Excel 'worksheet functions'.

This can be done with an expression similar to the following

```
value1 = Application.WorksheetFunction.FUNCTION_NAME()
```

for example

```
value1 = Application.WorksheetFunction.Norm_S_Dist(da, True)
```

3.14   Accessing data on a worksheet

Good programming practice suggests that a function should derive all the data that it needs from the values of its parameters.

However there are cases where you might need to access the values on a worksheet directly from within a macro function, such as when you need to search a table of values that appears on a worksheet.

The following example accesses the value in cell row 'r', column '2' on a worksheet directly.

```
Const MODELS_NAME as string = "Portfolios 15.12.16"

Const YIELDS as string = "Yields & MER"


value1 = Workbooks(MODELS_NAME).Worksheets(YIELDS).Cells(r, 2).Formula
```

If you want to use this method you will need to have the workbook open in Excel when you run the macro.

3.16   Running a macro from a separate worksheet

The above examples explain how to write a save a VBA macro within a workbook.

However you might wish to save a macro in a workbook and then run this macro from other workbooks.

This can be done by writing and saving the workbook that has the macro in it. Open this workbook in Excel, and make sure that you click on the 'Enable Macros' button if it appears when you open the workbook.

Then go to the new workbook that you are going to call the function from.

Click on the cell that you want to use to call the macro.

Click on the 'Fx' button on the menu bar.

This will bring up a dialog box.

Click on the 'Or select a category' drop-down list.

Scroll down and click on 'User defined'

You should now see a list of all available macros that you have written that are in open workbooks, and you can simply click on the appropriate one.

It is also possible to make macros permanently available by making your own Excel Add-in.

This is done by saving your macro workbook with a file type of "Excel Add-in"

Then go to

    File

Options

Add-Ins

Manage – Excel Add-ins – Go

And click on the name of your new Add-in file.

3.16   Debugging

When you are looking at a VBA code window, you can use the following shortcut keys for debugging the code.

F9   Inserts a 'breakpoint' on the line the cursor is on. Excel will stop executing the macro when it reaches this line, and you can examine the value of various variables.

Shift-F9   Displays the value of the variable that is highlighted by the cursor.

F8   Execute the line of code that the cursor is stopped on and step to the next line.

F5   Continue executing the macro after it has stopped, stopping only at the next breakpoint line or the end of the macro.

3.16   Error handling

By default, when a macro encounters an error, it simply stops without displaying any error message. This is not very helpful.

You can display an error message for errors by using the following code.

At the top of your function, add the following line of code

```
On Error GoTo err_code
```

At the end of your function, add the following code

```
Exit Function

err_code:

    MsgBox Err.Description
```

This code will have the effect of displaying an error message whenever the Excel macro encounters an error and stops.

3.16 Some useful functions

Some useful Excel VBA functions are listed below.

```
Open "c:\tmp\solutions.txt" For Output As #1
```

Opens a file for writing to. Ensure that the folder that you use is one that you have permission to write to.

```
Print #1, "shortest_path", shortest_path
```

Writes data out to your output file.

```
Close #1
```

Closes your output file.

```
MsgBox "Finished"
```

Displays a message in a box on the screen.

3.16 Writing your own functions and subroutines

As you write more complex and larger blocks of code, you will eventually have to break your VBA module files up into a number of functions and subroutines.

A subroutine is a block of code that you can call multiple times within your program.

It is declared in the following way

```
Private Sub your_sub_name( param1 as type1, param2 as type 2 )

    ` code here

End Sub
```

Replace the names within this definition with names that are appropriate to your code, and use however many parameters you need to.

To call the subroutine, simply place the name of the subroutine on a line by itself were you want to call it, as below

```
    your_sub_name( param1, param2)
```

A subroutine cannot return a value.

If you need a block of code that can return a value, use a private function instead.

This is declared in the following way

```
Private Function your_func_name( param1 as type1, param2 as type 2 )

    ` code here

    your_function_name = return_value

End Function
```

Replace the names within this definition with names that are appropriate to your code, and use however many parameters you need to.

To call the function, use the name of your function in an expression, as below.

```
    new_value = your_func_name( param1, param2 )
```

See the examples at the end of this book as a guide.

3.17   Good programming practice

Entire books can, and have, been written on good programming practice.

The author has written several books on programming and Computer Science for the interested reader.

However, Excel macros are usually written by practitioners in Finance, Social Sciences etc rather than professional programmers, so a few basic notes only may be in order.

Make sure that you lay out the code with plenty of blank lines between statements. This is extremely important and will ensure that a reader has some chance of understanding the code when they come back to work on it at a future date.
When you have an 'If' statement or 'While' loop, indent the code inside the statement by one tab stop. This is very important to enhance the readability of the code.

Include plenty of comments. You really can't have too many comments.

Don't use a variable to mean two different things inside a function. When this occurs declare two separate variables and use them separately.

Try to use names for variables that have some meaning. Avoid generic names such as 'x', y' ,'a' and 'b' unless they actually have some meaning in the context of the particular function.

4 Sample Excel macro code

4.1 Example 1 – Calculate the value of a 'call option'

```
' Calculate the premium (i.e. value) of a call option
'
' strike in dollars
' spot in dollars
' vol (volatility) as decimal volatility per year
' int_rate risk free interest rate in decimal per year
' days


Public Function call_premium(ByVal strike As Double, ByVal spot As Double, _
                             vol As Double, int_rate As Double, _
                             ByVal days As Double)

    Dim da As Double
    Dim db As Double

    spot = spot * 100
    strike = strike * 100
    days = days / 365

    da = (Log(spot / strike) + int_rate * days) / (vol * (days ^ 0.5)) + _
                                        0.5 * vol * (days ^ 0.5)

    db = da - vol * days ^ 0.5

    call_premium = spot * Application.WorksheetFunction.Norm_S_Dist(da, True) _
                        - strike * Exp(-int_rate * days) * _
                        Application.WorksheetFunction.Norm_S_Dist(db, True)


End Function
```

4.2 Example 2 – calculate the 'implied volatility of a call option'

```
' Calculate the Implied Volatility of a call option
'
' strike in dollars
' spot in dollars
' prem premium
' int_rate risk free interest rate in decimal per year
' days

Public Function call_implied_volatility(ByVal strike As Double, ByVal spot As Double, _

                                        ByVal prem As Double, int_rate As Double, _

                                        ByVal days As Double)

        Dim low As Double
        Dim high As Double
        Dim vol As Double
        Dim premium As Double
        Dim diff As Double
        Dim da As Double
        Dim db As Double

        spot = spot * 100
        strike = strike * 100
        days = days / 365

        low = 0
        high = 1
        vol = 0
        premium = 0
        diff = 100


        While (diff > 0.001 Or diff < -0.001)

            diff = premium - prem

            If premium > prem Then
                high = vol
                vol = low + (vol - low) / 2
            Else
                low = vol
                vol = vol + (high - vol) / 2
            End If

            da = (Log(spot / strike) + int_rate * days) / (vol * (days ^ 0.5)) + 0.5 * _
                                                    vol * (days ^ 0.5)

            db = da - vol * days ^ 0.5

            premium = spot * Application.WorksheetFunction.Norm_S_Dist(da, True) - _

                            strike * Exp(-int_rate * days) * _

                            Application.WorksheetFunction.Norm_S_Dist(db, True)
```

```
    Wend

    call_implied_volatility = vol

End Function
```

4.3 Example 3 – Search a table on a worksheet and return a value

```
Const MODELS_NAME As String = "Portfolios 17.11.2015.xlsm"

Const YIELDS As String = "Yields & MER"

'
' Return "Y" or "N" for if a security/fund has brokerage applied to it (i.e. yes for
listed securities, no for managed funds)
'

Public Function has_brokerage(security_fund As String) As String

    Dim r As Integer
    Dim found As Integer

    found = False
    has_brokerage = ""

    For r = 1 To 1000
       If Workbooks(MODELS_NAME).Worksheets(YIELDS).Cells(r, 2).Formula = _

            security_fund Or _

            Workbooks(MODELS_NAME). Worksheets(YIELDS).Cells(r, 3).Formula = _

            security_fund Then

          has_brokerage = Workbooks(MODELS_NAME). Worksheets(YIELDS).Cells(r, 4)

          found = True

       End If
    Next

    If Not found Then
        MsgBox security_fund & " not found"
    End If

End Function
```

4.1 Example 4 – Calculating tax (Australia)

```
' Calculate income tax for the 2015/16 financial year
'
' tax rates for 2015/16
' not applicable if the person is eligible for the seniors or pensioner's offset
(affects medicate levy)



Public Function calc_tax_2015_16(income As Double)

    Dim tax As Double

    If income > 180000 Then

        tax = 54547 + ((income - 180000) * 0.47)

    ElseIf income > 80000 Then

        tax = 17547 + ((income - 80000) * 0.37)

    ElseIf income > 37000 Then

        tax = 3572 + ((income - 37000) * 0.325)

    ElseIf income > 18200 Then

        tax = ((income - 18200) * 0.19)

    Else

        tax = 0

    End If


        ' medicare (single)

    If income > 26120 Then

        tax = tax + income * 0.02

    ElseIf income > 20897 Then

        tax = tax + (income - 20897) * 0.1

    End If

    calc_tax_2015_16 = tax

End Function
```

5 Resources

A number of websites have useful information for the VBA macro programmer.

You may refer to material on the author's personal website at www.markmcilroy.com

The site http://www.techonthenet.com/excel/formulas/ is very useful and has all Excel functions listed by category.

Pressing F1 in the Excel macro window will bring up the Microsoft help system. For help on a particular function or keyword, highlight the word before pressing F1.

6 About the author

Mark Laurence McIlroy has extensive experience working in the Financial Services sector in IT development roles, Portfolio Manager (Quantitative) and Financial Planning roles.

Mark has an undergraduate degree in Computer Science and Applied Mathematics.

Mark also as Masters degrees in Applied Finance and Financial Planning.

After a long career in Information Technology roles in the Financial Services sector in Australia, Mark has now made a career change into Financial Planning.

Mark lives with his wife in Melbourne, Australia.

Readers are welcome to send in general questions.

Mark can be contracted by email on mark.mcilroy@outlook.com

For further information please refer to the author's personal website at www.markmcilroy.com